# ENDORSE

"Somebody once said, 'There is something about the outside of a horse that is good for the inside of a man.' In today's world, there are two groups of people who, for many reasons, need to connect with a horse. Some are daunted by the prospect, and intimidation prevents them from touching such a thing of beauty. Others, through sheer enthusiasm, dive in headlong, not realizing what the impact could be for both themselves and their horses. The learning and sharing of experiences are the only ways that both of these groups can experience a little something of what horses can do for the inside of a person. This book can take you along that journey."

—Danny Cook and Gary Wells
Founders of *Animal 360*
*"Improving the welfare of animals through education"*

"The authors have done a great job of sharing their passion for horses and presenting relevant information. First time horse owners will benefit from the book's practical tips without feeling overwhelmed. Readers will be able to relate to each of the authors as they share their own experiences and development of their horsemanship."

—Chad R. Coppess
Professional trainer and founder of Cross Training Horsemanship
*www.graceadventures.org*

# YOU BOUGHT YOUR FIRST HORSE, NOW WHAT?

# YOU BOUGHT YOUR FIRST HORSE, NOW WHAT?

*A Book of Information and Inspiration for You and Your Horse*

JOAN FISCHER, LINDA GORDON, KARIN ROBERTS

TATE PUBLISHING
AND ENTERPRISES, LLC

Published by Tate Publishing & Enterprises, LLC
127 E. Trade Center Terrace | Mustang, Oklahoma 73064 USA
1.888.361.9473 | www.tatepublishing.com

Tate Publishing is committed to excellence in the publishing industry. The company reflects the philosophy established by the founders, based on Psalm 68:11, *"The Lord gave the word and great was the company of those who published it."*

Book design copyright © 2013 by Tate Publishing, LLC. All rights reserved.
*Cover design by Jan Sunday Quilaquil*
*Interior design by Caypeeline Casas*
*Cover photo and images by Linda Gordon*

Published in the United States of America

ISBN: 978-1-62510-285-0
1. Nature / Animals / Horses
2. Pets / Horses
14.02.28

# DEDICATION

*This book is dedicated to Sharon Neumeister who inspired us in a most peculiar way.*

# TABLE OF CONTENTS

# FOREWORD

So, you bought your first horse. Now, my friend, you are off on a fantastic journey. In the next few years, especially the first one, you're going to learn things about yourself that you had no clue were even there. Embrace the opportunity! Horses have the ability to make better people out of us.

You have taken on a tremendous, long-term responsibility, for horses do not come and go quickly. You must learn to care for him properly and daily. You do not get weekends off or paid vacation from your horse. You must educate yourself on how to take care of these responsibilities—feed, grooming, hoof care, tack—the list goes on. There are plenty of resources available to help you with all these things. Now you must educate yourself as to which of these are the best for you and your horse.

You will need help. Choose it carefully. Some of your choices are going to be poor ones. That's how you learn. As soon as you realize that you could have made a better choice—do so! I have dedicated my life to helping the horse get a better deal from the human, so I feel it is my responsibility to pass along just a few of the basic principles I've learned in the last fifty years. No small thanks goes to my friend and mentor, the late Ray Hunt.

First, a horse makes a great friend and companion, but a damn poor PET! A thousand pound pet will hurt you. He won't mean to, and there'll be no malice in it, but he'll hurt you just the same. Being hurt accidentally hurts just as bad as if it's done on purpose. Make a pet of him and before you know it you'll be pouring his feed over the fence because you're afraid to go in the pen with him. On the extreme end, you can make a thousand pound predator out of a horse.

Another way humans have trouble is relating to their horses in human terms. They are not human. They are a horse. Horses learn from birth to operate on a pecking order—dominance and submission. Neither of those words is bad. One is a leader and the other, the follower. God gave man "dominion" over the animals and with that comes a great responsibility. It's like a good dance partner. One leads and the other follows, but only by a fraction of a second. The only catch is that *you* have to learn to lead. If you don't, he will, and he sees nothing wrong with that. That's the only way he knows how to live. He's a horse.

Communication is of the utmost importance. That is not you telling or asking him to do something. Communication is the *exchange* of information between two entities. One-sided "communication" is a lecture. Ray always said that the horse is your best teacher. Learn to listen to him. He'll tell you where he needs help. Find out what's important to him and let that become important to you so things can work out.

Horses need discipline, but never punishment! Discipline is before or during the act. Punishment is after the act, and horses do *not* understand it! You must be fair, but firm. Your emotions should be left at the house—never brought to the barn. One of the greatest challenges of being a horseman is the ability to keep your emotions in check.

My goal is for everyone to get along with their horse. You and your horse don't have to go win a prize for you both to be winners. As long as you can go along and do whatever you do without trouble between you—there's the prize! You both win!

I'll leave you with this: early on I asked Ray to tell me something I could get ahold of as a goal or where I was headed with all this. He said, "I'll tell you what Tom (Dorrance) told me: 'The very first thing you need to know will be the last thing you learn.'" I said, "Well, that makes sense. Could you give me a hint as to what that might be?" He replied, "Honestly, I don't know yet!"

As I said, you are off on a fantastic journey. Embrace the challenge. Enjoy every step of the way!
Carpe Diem

Buster Mclaury
West Texas
www.bustermclaury.com

"*I hope you fall into good hands; but a horse never knows who may buy him, or who may drive him; it is all a chance for us...*"
*~ a wise mare's advice to her foal from the book,*
*Black Beauty by Anna Sewell 1877*

# I'VE ALWAYS WANTED A HORSE

### First and Foremost

You need to ask yourself if you have the time and energy to commit to horse ownership. This question should not be taken lightly. Horses are not hobbies. They are not something to be taken out and put away like a boat or motorcycle when the weather gets a little icky. They need your time and attention on a regular basis—rain or shine. Equine rescue facilities around the country are full to capacity because too many people did not consider these facts. If you think that you might not have the time to commit to horse ownership, share boarding or leasing could be an option for you.

### Shopping for a Horse

We should make this clear, shopping for a horse is *not* like a trip to the grocery store; however, making a list of needs and wants is a perfect way to start. I want a horse that looks like Black Beauty, but I need a horse that can take care of me and teach me to ride. If it looks a little like the old grey mare who, let's face it, ain't like she used to be having a bad hair day…so be it. She may just be the one who keeps you safe and out of the emergency room.

Where to find "the perfect horse," you ask? Here are just a few ideas: internet websites, newspapers, local boarding facilities, equine rescue facilities, herd dispersal sales, livestock auctions–the possibilities are endless. We've covered only a few, but you get the idea.

A good horse needs very little,
but he needs that very little a whole lot.

It's a great idea to bring someone along with some experience, someone who knows what to look for in a beginner's horse. If you are on your own in this endeavor, here are a few tips:

1.  Ask to be the one to handle the horse, even if you're not 100 percent comfortable handling horses just yet. Don't be intimidated, a patient horse and helpful seller will give you the time it takes for you to get familiar with the horse and gage his or her personality and behavior. You *will* need a patient horse to start out with. Often, first time horse owners seek an older experienced horse, while age does promote wisdom, it cannot be your only measuring stick. Sometimes a well-trained, well-treated younger horse is better than a twenty-year-old horse that has been poorly trained or mistreated.

2.  When you are looking at your prospective horse, here are some things to look for:
    Does the horse lead well, or does he seem to be completely oblivious to the fact that there is a human at the end of the lead rope? Has he tried to pull you into the next county? Does he constantly put his head down to eat grass? Is he willing to be led away from the barn, pasture, and/or his buddies, or is he breaking into a cold sweat, pawing, snorting, and calling for his pasture mates?

3.  Ask the owner to tack up the horse for you. While you're watching, be aware of the horse's body language. Are the ears pinned, tail swishing, dancing the hokeypokey in the aisle? All of these are signs that the horse is *not* happy about something. Is he cinchy? When the girth is pulled too tight too quickly, it can cause the horse to become aggressive, irritated, and unwilling to be saddled. You might also ask the owner to show you that the horse allows all of its feet to be handled with ease.

4.  Ask the owner to ride the horse for you so you can observe his attitude, gait, and willingness. If someone is going to go flying through the air (also called "unplanned dismount"), let it be the owner. It's a good idea to see the horse walk, trot, and canter. Of all the gaits, the trot is where most lameness issues will show up. If you are buying a trail horse, see if the owner would consider taking a short drive with you to a local horse park or a trailhead to gauge the behavior of the horse outside of his comfort zone. First, go ahead and meet the owner at their barn, and watch while the horse is being loaded onto the trailer. It should not take all day or ten people to successfully get the horse in the trailer.

## ~ Tanya Newkirk

I can remember the day I got my first horse. I was not accustomed to getting "big" birthday presents, but that is exactly what I got when I turned ten. A 900 pound present to be exact! I completely fell for the story about my dad going to get ice cream or something, but when he drove up with a horse, I'm sure I was speechless! Now I know that in today's world of beautiful horse trailers with nicer living accommodations than my home, to mention that my horse came home in the back of a pickup probably brings up images of The Beverly Hillbillies! Before you panic too much, the truck did have a high enclosure that went around the bed and she managed to handle the short trip just fine. Bambi was a Morgan-Welch mare and a tri-color paint to boot. What more could a ten year old horse adoring girl ask for? That was the start of a lifelong love of horses for me. I am sure that my parents shared more information than comes to mind, but for the most part I remember learning how to saddle, bridle, stop, turn and go. At that point I was free to hit the trails – or woods and pastures. Trainers? Lessons? Seriously. It was, "Here she is, now go have fun and be careful." In all my years of riding her, there was only once when I managed to come off.

All horses deserve, at least once in their lives, to be loved by a little girl.

That probably had more to with me breaking some speed record than any fault of the horse. She was my companion, entertainment, love and therapist all wrapped up in one. I spent countless hours riding, grooming and learning how to care for a horse. She was such a blessing to me. I did end up selling her to some friends when I was in college and have been fortunate to have been blessed with a wonderful husband who has graciously allowed me to continue this addiction. Today we currently have a herd of six, including, of course, a paint mare. I have converted to the more traditional form of horse transportation today but am forever grateful for my dad's willingness to bring Bambi home in whatever fashion needed to accomplish the job.

"*Whoever said money can't buy happiness, didn't know where to buy a horse.*"

# I OWN A THOUSAND POUND ANIMAL...
# NOW WHAT?

All of us, at one point or another, have experienced the feelings that come with owning our first horse—excitement, fear, trepidation, feelings of inadequacy—we want to share with you how horses first came into our lives.

———————

## ~ *Joan Fischer*

When I was ten years old, I asked for a horse for Christmas. What I received that year was a giant Habitrail and two hamsters. I named them Milla and Clara after my two grandmothers. They never said anything, but I always got the feeling that being named after a rodent didn't thrill or flatter them in any way. While somewhat disappointed that a horse wasn't under the tree, the reality was being one of six children, with your father being a school teacher, and your mom was a stay-at-home mom, as they all were back then, hamsters fit the budget.

"Why buy the cow when you can get the milk for free?" describes, I am sure, my parent's train of thought. My auntie Frankie was a short ten minute drive away, and her little hobby farm was filled with all the livestock animals a wannabe country girl could hope for. At one time, I believe, she was up to eleven horses. There were cows, goats, a pig who thought she was a German Shepherd, chickens to pluck...you get the idea. There was also a *sweet* little pony named Tammi for me to ride.

Tammi, being your typical pony, had a little attitude and plenty of her own ideas. She did not like double riders, so what would my cousin Kris and I do? Jump on her and ride her double. She would start rearing and bucking; we would laugh, and Auntie Frankie would yell at us to get off of her. As an adult, the last thing I want is a horse to buck, and I take great care in training my horses to avoid any bucking. Experience, wisdom that comes with age, and the fact that the ground is a lot harder these days has given me a strong desire to stay safely in the saddle. Tammi would also lay down when she didn't want to give us rides anymore. She learned the quickest way back to the pasture was to start lying down.

I grew up, went off to college, got a job, met my husband, and had three children. One year for Christmas, guess what my husband, Dave, gave me? A horse! Twenty six years after I asked for that first horse, I finally received her. Never give up on your dreams.

# ~ *Linda Gordon*

I grew up in a suburb of Chicago where bikes, roller skates, and skateboards were what all of us kids rode everyday. I didn't know anybody that had horses, not even a distant relative. I had miles of sidewalks to ride my bike, the neighborhood park to meet up with friends, and my favorite climbing tree in the front yard. At ten years old, a family vacation to Colorado changed my life. As we made the long drive from Illinois to the Rocky Mountains, I watched the landscape change from the window of the back seat of the station wagon. Wide open prairies, rolling hills, and farmland stretched across the horizon, and I had never seen anything more beautiful. My first trail ride was through Garden of the Gods in Colorado Springs, and that was it. I was on a rocky mountain high, and I never wanted to come down. The rest of the trip seemed like a dream, and I would spend the rest of my childhood wearing hiking boots, singing John Denver songs, painting mountains, drawing horses, and photographing everything in sight. I found a livery stable that, as luck would have it, was at the end of a pleasant ten-mile ride down the bike trails through the county forest preserve. I cleaned stalls for free for the privilege of being around horses. I spent five years riding seasoned, sometimes stubborn trail horses on weekends during school and everyday in the summer until I needed a real paying job.

Life went on, jobs came and went; I adopted a little girl, and got married. Still living in the suburbs of Chicago, horses didn't have a place in my busy life, but photography had become a passion rather than a hobby and, eventually, a career. Our little family moved a little further from the city to a five-acre piece of paradise in an equine community. Just down the road from our place was a horse rescue farm, and once again I found myself cleaning stalls for free for the privilege of being around horses. I continued to volunteer for the next five years, and in that time, I adopted two young horses of my own. Until the day I brought them home, I thought I knew all I needed to know about horses—was I ever wrong! They had never been trained, but I thought, with all the love and nurturing I would give them, they would just become the horses of my dreams. A few minor bumps and bruises later, I knew I needed help. I found *Downunder Horsemanship* with Clinton Anderson on RFD-TV, and a whole new world of horsemanship opened up to me. I soaked up every bit of knowledge this horseman from Australia had to offer. I studied other clinicians as well, but found that Clinton Anderson's' method worked for me and my horses. I packed up my camera gear and attended one of his tour stops in Des Moines, Iowa, in 2007, and became completely inspired to bring my horsemanship to a new level, and made a new goal for myself: to become a photographer for *Downunder Horsemanship*.

My horsemanship goals were realized somewhat quicker than my new career goal. With consistent work and patience, my two rescue horses did become the horses of my dreams. In September of 2010, I became the road staff photographer for *Downunder Horsemanship*.

# ~ *Karin Roberts*

So you bought yourself a horse, now what? Good, bad, or otherwise your new best friend will forever be embedded in your memory from here on. Allow me to share with you how my first horse was a very good experience for me. She taught me firsthand how much I really didn't know about horses.

Penny was a twelve-year-old quarter horse mare being sold at the barn my friend owned. She was older, I didn't have to move her, and she was within my budget. She also came with an English saddle, and a box full of all sorts of fun horsey things. One-stop shopping just the way I like it!

It didn't bother me that Penny was a "cribber" and had to wear some sort of gizmo around her neck so she wouldn't suck air in her stall. All I wanted to do was ride, and she had perfect ground manners, which was an asset to me at the time. I had no idea how a halter was applied, let alone how to groom, pick feet, or tack up a horse in any discipline. She would stand in the crossties for what seemed like hours while I tried to figure out if I had the saddle on correctly.

Penny loved to be groomed and fussed over. By no means, was she perfect, but boy was she smart. Penny's previous owner would ride her in the arena for twenty minutes at a time. No more, no less. Penny also trained me to do the same by stopping at the gate and refusing to give me any more work after her twenty minutes were up. Of course, I gave in to her antics because she was probably tired. After all, what did I know? I was just relieved that I had stayed on her back for twenty minutes!

After a while, I decided arena work was not for me, so Penny and I hit the trail. Boy, those days were a blast! I thought that all horses were supposed to jump over water, puddles, ditches, and bolt as fast as they could on the way back to the barn. It only took a few group rides before I noticed that the other horses in the group didn't do such things. I later learned that it was considered "bad behavior." But that's okay. I enjoyed my time on her back all the same. Penny loved trail riding in a group so much that in no time at all, she was sporting a pretty red ribbon on her tail. I spent most of my trail rides in the last position and could never hear any of the fun stories my friends were telling.

To me, all of that was no big deal and really kind of fun. That was ten years ago, and I have continued to learn so much more about horses and horsemanship.

Once you've been bitten by the horse bug, you may find yourself adding to your little herd. Joan has found a great method for introducing a new horse to the group. The newest member of the family is separated from the herd by a fence line, for at least a day, to establish familiarity with his or her new herd mates. This allows the horse to observe the herd's pecking order without becoming a victim of the "boss mare." Spreading piles of hay at the fence line, so that all of the horses can reach it, enables the horses to "break bread," and touch noses across the fence in a non-threatening way. Horses whose heads are lowered are in a relaxed state, and using the hay as a tension breaker gives them something to do together other than fight for dominance over the fence. At night, Joan brings the horses into their own stalls, so they can relax in their own space. The new horse can rest comfortably after a long day of making new friends. She likes to do this for one or two days, but that will depend on your herd and their behavior and their acceptance of the new member. If you can read a horse's body language, this will help you to foresee where this horse will fit into the pecking order and take precautions as necessary.

The day you turn the herd out together for the first time, you'll want to put them in an area that they have the most space available, not an area that has corners and places for one horse to trap another. Put your new horse out first, then the boss mare, and down the pecking order. Now stand back, and watch them integrate. Do not get caught in the middle of a skirmish, it might happen, but it's natural and its okay. It will be over in a short amount of time, and all will be right in their world.

The herd's first reaction to the
introduction of a new horse

The lead mare is establishing her
dominance of the herd.

Curiosity drives the horses to offer a tentative
greeting with the exchange of breath.

As seen here, the group has settled and
feels less threatened by the newcomer.

# Husband Horse – (noun)

The horse entrusted to keep the non-riding husband safe when they are so inclined to join us on the trail. This happens infrequently when the golf game is cancelled, the fish aren't biting, and all other sporting events are not televised that day. In some cases, a spouse just isn't up for riding at all, but Bob has become an excellent "horse-and mini-mule sitter" when Linda is on the road with *Downunder Horsemanship*.

Dave Fischer and Arizona

Bob Gordon and Allie

Tom Roberts and Sadie

The wind of heaven...is that which blows between a horse's ears

# COMMUNICATION AND RESPECT
## R-E-S-P-E-C-T—FIND OUT WHAT IT MEANS TO ME!

The first thing you need to understand about the horse is that it is a very large, strong, thinking animal. As a horse handler you have to know that you are not going to out-muscle him—because you can't. You need to gain his respect. You have to become the "lead mare," so to speak. You are thinking "great…how do I do that?" We're getting to that. Your horse is looking for leadership, and if you do not provide that for them they will take over the reins.

*"Do not go where the path may lead, go instead where there is no path and leave a trail."*

*—Ralph Waldo Emerson*

Horses are followers; but if you don't lead, they will.

We would be remiss if we did not stress the fact that the safety of you and your horse is the first and most important matter at hand.

Our goal is to help you learn to understand your horse, not put on you the golden path to winning blue ribbons at the state fair.

Understanding the horse's behavior and body language comes naturally to some people, and does not to others. If you are someone who isn't a natural horse whisperer, don't worry. There are many professional clinicians out there who can help you develop a safe plan for you and your horse, and put you on the right track to becoming lifelong partners.

My favorite clinician is Clinton Anderson of *Downunder Horsemanship*. You can find more information about his method at: www.downunderhorsemanship.com.

*"Understanding the horse, as opposed to making him understand us."*
—Frederic Pignon

# Human nature

When a child is frightened by something, our basic instinct is to offer comfort, a soft touch, a soothing voice assuring the child that everything is going to be all right. With horses however, singing lullabies and cooing sweet nothings in their ears will not offer them comfort, but instead reassures them that whatever has just spooked them, is indeed going to devour them in an instant. Here's a common scenario:

Your nice Saturday afternoon trail ride is suddenly interrupted by some litterbug's grocery sack wafting along on the breeze, a branch laying across the trail that was not there yesterday, a killer boulder, or pack of weekend-warrior mountain bikers wearing those very trendy cyclist outfits (should some of these people really be wearing spandex? C'mon, you've all wondered the same thing; we're just saying it out loud). Quite honestly, a horse can just up and bolt,* and you'll never know the reason why. However, the groundwork and desensitizing exercises will help to make these occurrences far less frequent.

So, what do you do when your horse is upset? First *you* stay calm. This is not easy but it comes with experience. Encourage your horse's feet to move and focus on the task at hand. There's no shame in getting off of your horse if you are uncomfortable gaining control from in the saddle. Sometimes, working from the ground is the best place to remind your horse that you are still there and in control.

Do not allow the horse to stop and focus on the object of its fear. Once his full attention is on the object of anxiety, he has no recollection that there is a rider on his back. You are a distant memory, if that, and soon you may find yourself separated from your mount.

*It's a lot like nuts and bolts - if the rider is nuts, the horse bolts.*

—*Nicholas Evans*

---

\* **Bolt.** (verb)—The very fastest that your horse can stop, turn, spin, and accelerate before you can even utter an expletive.

# Establishing Leadership

You must play the part of the confident horse person even if you don't feel that way at first, you'll get there. If you appear unsure, timid, and uncertain, your horse will pick up on these body signals and assume you are not lead mare extraordinaire.*

To become the leader, you should walk with your shoulders back, head up, and eyes forward. Approach your horse or horses with confidence, but not like a predator. Every horse will try to test their boundaries, they will do what they can to push you around, invade your space, step on you, or even bite you to make you move. Your horse should always face you and give you its full attention. If you are staring into the business end of your equine, you are not the first and foremost thing on his mind. To keep your horses attention, give him a job.**

Horses already know how to establish leadership. They understand the pecking order, and each is mindful of his position in the herd. The mares teach their young respect and spacial relationships early on in life. Therefore, when the horse exhibits some of the above mentioned behaviors, they are trying to establish dominance over you. Natural horsemanship isn't about whispering to horses some magical spell that instantly makes them understand what you want them to do. It is about learning to adopt and use inherent equine behaviors to achieve true leadership in their eyes. In the "Seventh Stall" we will get into how you can accomplish this with consistent groundwork and confident handling of your horse.

---

\*   Lead Mare Extraordinaire—Now and then, you meet a horse that is the dominant horse of the herd. It's almost always a mare unless she forfeits that job to a gelding. Joan's mare, Cheyenne, is *The* Lead Mare Extraordinaire in any herd situation she encounters. Cheyenne exudes confidence and has a presence about her that quietly communicates her dominance among other horses. This is the kind of body language and air of confidence you need to become the lead mare extraordinaire of your own herd.

\*\*  A job in this case doesn't involve punching the time clock and picking up a check on the first and fifteenth of every month. A job simply means keeping your horse's feet and mind busy."

## ~ *Jean Adams*

I've been a horse owner for years and have a special appreciation for Clydesdales. I have ridden Clydes, driven them, and I love their sweet, gentle nature. I had one particular experience that really taught me to think like a horse. I was moving Glen out of the pasture when he suddenly stopped in the middle of the open gate—on my foot. I couldn't get him to move forward or backward no matter what I did. I pushed, pulled, yanked, and yelled to no avail. The other horses in the pasture were beginning to eye the open gate, and I was firmly planted in place by 2500 pounds of my sweet, loveable Clydesdale. All I could think to do was lean over and bite him right in the shoulder. That got his attention! He moved over about as quickly as a Clyde can move, released my foot, and we got through the gate without the rest of the herd. I had to laugh later that evening while I was flossing horse hair out of my teeth.

# One Smart Horse

## ~ *Cherylyn A.*

At our farm many years ago, we used electric fencing to separate the paddocks, but we didn't always keep the electric turned on. Our quarter horse Mindy is a smart horse, and it was at grain time we realized just how clever she is. If I was doing the feeding, to avoid getting zapped by the fence, I would call out to Rob, "is the electric turned on?" He would either call out yes or no. Mindy learned the meaning of the words pretty quickly. If the answer was no, she would squeeze through the fence and eat the other horses grain. If the answer was yes, it meant the electric was turned on, and she would stay in her own paddock. Once we figured out she understood what yes and no meant, we had to start spelling out the words so that she would stay in her own paddock. As smart as Mindy is, she never learned to spell!

*At its finest, rider and horse are joined not by tack, but by trust. Each is totally reliant upon the other. Each is the selfless guardian of the others very well-being.*

*~Fourth Stall~*

# DON'T FENCE ME IN

Where will you keep your horse? There are boarding facilities if you don't have enough space on your property for a barn and pastures or paddocks. If that is the route you'll take, here are a few things to keep in mind. Are the horses turned out daily on pasture or dry lot? Find out the ratio of horses per acre. Overcrowding leads to injuries, intestinal parasites and lack of forage. What kind of shelter is there, a barn with stalls, or run-in sheds? Or, heaven forbid, will your horse be stuck in a box stall, only to be allowed out when you visit the barn in your free time. Even if you go to the barn everyday for a couple hours, that is great dedication, but your horse still ends up standing for twenty-two hours a day. Let's take a look at the wild horses and the way they live.

Wild horses average twenty–thirty miles of travel per day. Horses, wild or domestic, are herd animals. The constant travel is nature's way of keeping them healthy and fit. A wild horse's hooves are simply perfect. They are trimmed, not by their local farrier, but by the terrain. As they travel, they graze. The constant search for forage is what drives them forward and sustains their survival.

Are you going to keep your horse at home on an established horse farm? Or will you get to start the place from the ground up? When planning out your horse property keep in mind the needs of your equine, and also try to make the set up easy for you. Fencing, moving horses, feeding, and cleaning are some things to consider when designing your space. When planning your pasture or paddock layout, try to create rectangular spaces, rather than square fenced areas. Horses are more likely to move freely when they don't feel boxed in. A nice, long, rectangle-shaped paddock is conducive to encouraging longer strides when your horse gets frisky.

# Fencing

The variety of fencing available out there might require another book, but we want you to know that there are some that are more economical than others, and that safety, again, is the most important thing to consider as well as maintenance.

A horse ain't bein' polite when he comes to the fence and lets you go over first.

# ~ *Linda Gordon*

The wild horse of the American West, untamed and free. I am always amazed by their sharp instincts; alert and ready to flee when they notice my presence. Nostrils flare, ears prick forward as they stand motionless in the vast desert. I've learned not to behave as a predator, to give them time to understand that I am no threat. I don't approach them directly and often look down at the ground. I watch their muscles relax, lower their heads as the lead mare sends the signal to the herd that they are safe. In just a few minutes, the silence of the desert is filled with the gentle sound of soft nickers as they continue to forage for the sparse grasses beneath the sage.

# Moving horses—"Git along, little doggy. Git along"

When you are moving your horses from one pasture to another, it's easier if you have pastures that are divided by fencing and gates, rather than leading them from paddock to pasture and back again. It's a matter of designing the space you have available effectively, creating accessibility from one area to another by fences, gates, and/or runs. If you have four or five horses, you don't want to have to lead two or four at a time from one area to another. This is time consuming and can be dangerous if one of your horses spooks or decides he would like to go somewhere else and take you and his buddies along for the ride.

# Water Source—Belly up to the bar, or tank as it were.

Clean fresh water must be available for your horses at all times. There are automatic waterers, stock tanks, and natural water sources. Horses should drink ten to twelve gallons of water per day. The more horses drink, the healthier they are. Dehydration leads to colic, which we will cover in the "Sixth Stall." If you use a stock tank in winter, depending on the climate in which you live, your tank will freeze over if it doesn't have a tank heater. That being said, you need to have electricity near your water tank. Of course, there are some people who don't have an electric source near their tank and must be diligent about going out four or five times a day to break the ice. This isn't an ideal situation but, if it's absolutely necessary, it can be done. Mineral and salt blocks encourage your horse to drink more water, and it's a good idea to keep these blocks available year round.

# Feeding—"Strappin' on the feed bag"

The best way to come up with a feeding schedule for your horse is to contact your local large animal vet, extension service, or a feed company and do some research. Depending on the breed of horse you have, the dietary requirements will be different. Here are some general guidelines:

A good rule of thumb is to feed one pound of hay per day for every hundred pounds of weight. A thousand pound horse would be fed ten pounds of hay per day. Three factors that determine the amount of hay your horse needs are: climate, quality of hay (grass, alfalfa, pasture mix); and the breed, health, or the age of your horse. There are grains and supplements that can be added to their diet, and that is for you to decide based on what kind of horse you have and what his or her dietary needs are. If you have the time and are at home during the day, it's a good idea to feed smaller portions more often than two big meals a day. A horse's digestive system is built to take in small amounts throughout the day.

# Cleaning—Here's the scoop on poop

The average one-thousand-pound horse produces approximately fifty pounds of manure per day. Let's take a moment to ponder that. Per horse, there will be at least seven piles of poop, deposited for you to pick up each day. (How many horses did you say you wanted?) In truth, some people find cleaning the barn, picking up the paddock very enjoyable. It's time spent with your horses, in your barn and a good opportunity to observe the horses interact with one another. It also gives them the opportunity to observe you. Not to mention the awesome upper body strength you'll develop. Okay, there are those (like Karin) who do not enjoy this particular task. If wearing muck boots and hauling excrement isn't your cup of tea, or bucket of manure, there will be other opportunities to bond with your equines. Whether you choose to do it yourself or hire someone to get it done for you, manure management is an important part of your daily routine.

*"The horse... if God made anything more beautiful,*
*He kept it for Himself"*

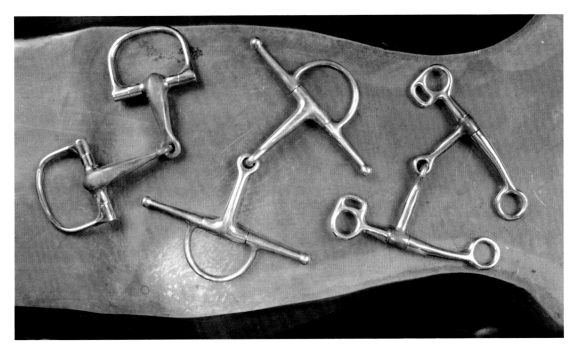

*~Fifth Stall~*

# TOOLS, EQUIPMENT, AND GADGETS...OH MY!

You walk into your tack shop because you need some equipment. Aisles and aisles of merchandise...where do you start? Let's start at the top with the halter and lead rope.

## Halters

You will find several different types of halters to choose from, it's only a matter of preference. There are nylon webbed, rope, and leather halters. If you are going to leave a halter on your horse, you should be sure that the halter is what is called a break-away halter. If the horse gets caught on something, as he pulls to free himself, a leather strap will break away and free the horse before he injures himself. Rope halters do not come with break-away straps, they are not meant to leave on your turned-out horse. Rope halters are designed to give you additional leverage with knots placed at the pressure points on the horse's nose. These are ideal for ground work and training.

# Lead Ropes

Lead ropes come in all materials and lengths. Shorter lengths can be dangerous and, for the most part, ineffective. For ground tying and training, lengths from fourteen to twenty feet keep the horse a safe distance from you. You don't need one thousand pounds on top of you...well...ever. When your horses are safe and they respect you as a leader, you can invite them into your personal space. If they are going to get goofy or spooky, let them do that at the end of a long lead rope. We prefer a good heavy marine quality rope with leather poppers on the end.

# Saddles

Once you have decided which riding discipline you prefer—English, western, dressage, endurance—that will determine what type of saddle you purchase, you can spend a little or a whole lot. There are synthetics and leather or a combination of both. Ultimately, your budget will dictate your purchase. Go in with a purchase price in mind, and stick with it. Yes, saddles are pretty, but most importantly they need to fit you as a rider and fit your horse. If you need a seventeen-inch saddle and try to squeeze your fanny into a fifteen–inch—yes, that saddle will make your butt look big.

Fitting your saddle to your horse is the most important issue. An improper fit can cause your horse discomfort and/or pain, which can lead to back problems and, quite possibly, bad behavior. To get a proper fit you need to know several things. Let's start with the withers.

Does your horse have high withers? Is he mutton withered or somewhere in between? Your horse's withers will determine what height the pommel of your saddle needs to be. The pommel should never come in contact with the back of the horse. Now that you figured out the withers, take a look at the barrel.

A wider horse would require full quarter horse bars for a good comfortable fit while a narrow, more slender-barreled horse would do well with semi-quarter horse bars. The gullet measurement of the saddle can help determine if the saddle is too wide or narrow for your horse. There will be at least one person in your tack shop who can help you find the perfect fit. If you are unsure, don't be afraid to *ask questions*. We are only scraping the surface on types of saddles, but we really wanted to stress the point that saddle fit matters.

## *Calculating Western-Cinch Size*

Measure the heart girth, divide that by two, and subtract three inches. This will give you the size of the cinch you'll need to fit your horse properly. The heart girth is measured from the base of the withers down to a couple of inches behind the horse's front legs, under the belly, then up the opposite side to where you started. The correct placement of the cinch is important to maintain a comfortable fit and balanced position of the saddle.

(We would like to thank the Golden Horseshoe in Eureka, Missouri, for the use of the grooming equipment pictured above.)

# PARTS OF A SADDLE

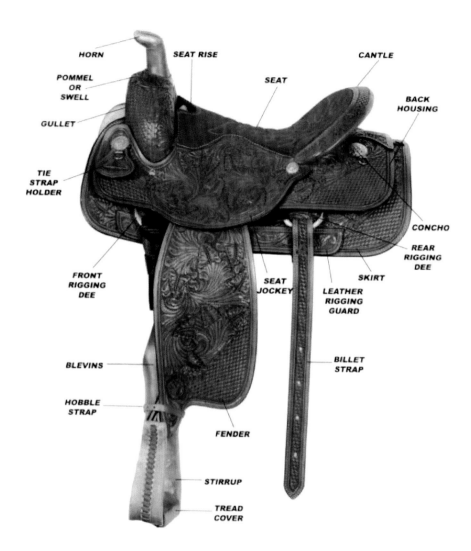

*Saddle Pads*

Saddle pads come in all shapes, colors, and sizes and can help your saddle fit the horse. Wool is a really good choice. It breathes and is a natural material that lasts a long time. Fleece pads are nice, but don't last as long and tend to get lumpy with use. Again, there are many pads to choose from but you will choose what works for your horse and your budget. Most importantly, before you use the saddle pad be sure it is clean and free of debris, and dry it thoroughly after each use.

Arizona is wearing a western bridle with a brow band, throat latch, and Tom thumb bit generally used for neck reining.

Tacoda is sporting a hackamore bit which works off the pressure points along the horse's nose.

Cheyenne is modeling the one eared western bridle. Notice there is no throat latch or brow band.

"Half the failures in life arise from pulling in ones horse as he is leaping."

—Agustus Hare

Here, Tacoda is showing off a standard-English bridle with a cavesson style noseband and D ring snaffle bit used for direct reining.

*"...or would you rather be a mule..."*

# SIGNS, SIGNALS AND SYMPTOMS

Here is some basic information on common health concerns.

There are five main signs of health that an owner is reasonably able to assess on a regular basis: Body temperature, heart or pulse rate, respiratory rate, temperament, and feeding pattern. The normal average temperature should be 101–101.5 degrees °F, anything above 102 is a problem. How do you take a horses temperature? Do we have to say *not* to try to put a thermometer under his tongue? Gosh! I hope not. Rectally is the only way to go.

The pulse rate of a horse at rest is around forty beats per minute. If the pulse rate is sixty or higher in a resting horse, there could be something wrong, call your vet. Stethoscopes can be purchased at a local medical supply company. If you don't have a stethoscope, you can locate your horses pulse by placing a finger over the bottom edge of the lower jaw and about half way along the jaw.

Temperament and feeding are up to you to determine. You can usually tell if your horse isn't feeling well if you notice a change in behavior or routine, not wanting to eat their grain, or acting lethargic. You will get to know your horse's routines and habits once you've spent some time together.

*Colic* is an incredibly serious situation for your horse and requires immediate attention from you and your vet. Colic is severe abdominal pain that can be triggered by different things. Some causes of colic are a disruption to normal bowel movements or changes in diet and routine. Some horses can get so upset that it sets off an episode of colic. We don't always know the causes, but most importantly, you must be able to recognize the symptoms and act quickly. Other than the visible symptoms, you can listen to the belly for gurgling noises in the digestive tract. If you hear nothing, you might also see some other indicators. Here are a few signs to look for:

1. Horse may stand and look back at its flank
2. The horse may also kick at its flank
3. Repeatedly laying down and rolling
4. Refusing food, even treats

In the winter, if you live in a colder climate, it's likely your horse is eating more hay due to snow covered pastures. Grass not only contains nutrients, but also moisture. Lack of water in the digestive tract causes the hay to become "stuck" and creates blockage. Salt and mineral blocks are going to encourage your horse to drink plenty of water throughout the year. In winter, keep your water tanks heated to just above freezing. Ice cold water is not desirable to horses, and going outside three to four times a day to chop ice isn't any fun for you either.

# De-worming

Parasites of all kinds can cause immeasurable damage if not prevented by keeping up a regular de-worming schedule. You can ask your vet, local extension program, and research on-line; there are several products available. Control measures should start in your paddock. Keep it free of manure. You should clean your paddocks daily. It cuts down on flies, odor, and all kinds of parasites. If you have a harrow, you can drag your pastures which breaks up the feces, exposing the eggs to the air and sun which dries out the egg effectively killing them. Routinely picking up your pastures is a good idea. The key here is that all around cleanliness and good horse health go hand in hand.

## Friendly Tip when De-worming:

Always remember to remove the cap of the de-wormer before injecting the paste into your horse's mouth. Silly suggestion you say? Ask Casper, Joan's Tennessee Walking Horse. He will tell you, if he could speak, how hard it is to separate the plastic cap floating around in his mouth from the paste. A normally easy going horse to de-worm, Casper was making the facial expressions of an old toothless cowboy on the range, about to hack up a wad of chewing tobacco. Joan didn't quite understand what was going on until the plastic cap was catapulted out of Casper's mouth and shot clear across the barn. Good boy that he is, he didn't spit out the paste, just the cap. Everyone forgets from time to time, and you will have plenty of silly stories of your own to share as time goes by—you'll see. Laugh at yourself, nothing is the end of the world and it's all about learning along the way.

Ever wonder what your horse weighs? We have a formula to figure it out, as follows:

Multiply the heart girth × the heart girth × length of the horse. Divide by three hundred and subtract fifty.

Proper length measurement of the horse—start at the middle of the chest, around the side of the horse, to the middle of the tail. This length measurement will also be how you determine what size blanket will fit your horse.

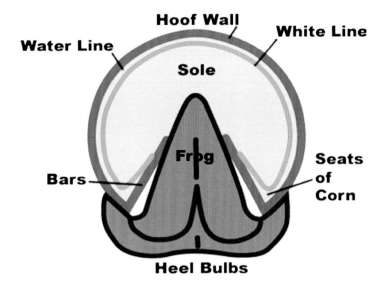

Hoof Wall—Outer part of the horses hoof.

White Line—Inner part of the horses hoof.

Water Line—Built up by the coronet and the walls. It is very resistant to contact with the ground and serves mainly as a support function.

Bars—Inward folds of the walls.

Seats of Corn—The sole between heel walls and bars used by farriers to evaluate correct heal height.

Frog—Dark grey in color and of a rubbery consistency, suggesting its role as shock absorber and grip tool on hard surfaces. The frog acts as a pump to move the blood back to the heart.

Sole—Covers the space from the hoof walls to the bars and the frog.

# Hoofin' it

A healthy hoof is a happy horse. Let's move on down to the feet. We've all heard the saying, "No hoof, no horse". Well, it's absolutely true. We are going to give you a few things to consider seasonally.

*Laminitis (grass founder)* is triggered by too high a level of carbohydrates in the stomach. Laminitis is the lameness of all four feet. Researchers have identified *fructan*, a carbohydrate similar to starch found primarily in "cool season" grasses such as fescue, timothy, and orchard grasses as the culprit. Fructan cannot be digested in the foregut, but it ferments rapidly in the hindgut. In large amounts, this causes a buildup of lactic acid, which kills off the bacteria in the gut that releases *endotoxins* into the blood. These endotoxins affect the cardiovascular system, restricting the flow of oxygen and nutrients to the feet. The *laminae* become inflamed, and some cells are killed off, weakening the structures of the hoof. A horse is most likely to founder in spring or fall in cooler climates when the nights cool down but the days warm up. People used to think that the overweight horse that grazed on the lush grass of spring was the cause, but research has shown the concentrated levels of sugar in the grass is the real problem. The grass will store a lot of the sugar at the base of the blade when the weather is cool. As the temperature increases, it tells the grass to release the sugar to the top of the blade. Horses graze and 'trim' the tops of the blades of grass, ingesting too much fructan.

*Thrush* is an infection, which usually affects the softer areas of the frog, but other parts of the hoof can be affected as well. There is a foul odor that you'll notice when picking your horses feet if he is infected by thrush. Some causes include standing in wet urine soaked stalls or standing outside in mud for long periods of time. This is easily prevented by keeping your horses feet clean and dry. Thrush can make a horse lame, remember our saying? "Healthy hoof, happy horse!"

Unrelated to the hoof, but directly related to moisture, *rain scald* (rain rot) is an infection of the skin on the upper surfaces of the horse's body caused by trapped moisture under the hair. A sign of rain scald are raw areas of the skin which start out very small, and scabs form. Bacteria from the sores can be transferred from one horse to another by using the same brushes or saddle pads. This is one of those things that can be prevented by regularly grooming your horse. If it's been wet for long stretches of time, go out now, and then towel dry the hair. Fluff the hair up to allow the air to dry the short guard hairs underneath. If you make a habit of good grooming practices, any little scabs appear, you'll be able to spot them right away and treat the affected area with an antiseptic spray or shampoo. An ounce of prevention is worth a pound of cure!

A very informative book you might want to pick up is called *What's Wrong with My Horse?* by Colin J. Vogel.

Another fantastic reference is a new Iphone app: Horse 360–More information on this must have: www.horse360.com.au

# Growth

Hoof growth occurs from the coronary band down towards the toe.

The average hoof grows one-fourths to three-eighths inch per month.

The average hoof is three to four inches in length; essentially, the horse grows a new hoof every year.

Rapidly growing hooves are considered to be a higher quality and easier to keep properly trimmed and/or shod.

Four factors that affect hoof growth are: age, season, structural injury or irritation, and nutrition.

# Age

Hoof growth can be directly correlated to the hearth rate. Young horses have a higher heart rate than older horses. They also have a faster rate of growth in their hooves.

However, older horses that are highly conditioned and have a slower heart rate have been found to have faster hoof growth. Exercise offsets the effect of the slower heart rate.

# Season

A horse's hoof will grow faster in the spring of the year than in any other season. Cool, damp weather, and the fact that they are no longer growing hair, the body puts the energy toward hoof growth. It slows dramatically in the winter.

# Structure

Systemic fever or injury of the sensitive structures results in rapid hoof growth.

# Nutrition

Proper nutrient intake stimulates maximum hoof growth. Biotin supplementation is suggested to improve hoof growth over time. It takes several months of feeding, and growth is most affected and best aided with proper nutrition and feeding a properly balanced ration.

*"To many, the words love, hope and dreams are synonymous with horses."*
*~ Oliver Wendell Holmes, Sr.*

# FROM THE GROUND UP

Groundwork is a term usually associated with equine clinicians or what people do when they are working with young horses. There are many clinicians out there with methods that will help you become confident with your horse, on the ground, and under saddle. Let's clarify things. Groundwork establishes respect, trust, and builds upon your status as leader. By working with your horse on the ground, you are working towards building a partnership with your horse. One misconception is that groundwork is used to "tire the horse out before you ride." Chasing your horse around an arena or round pen is only conditioning your horse physically, and teaching him to run from you. If this is the method your friends are using, for the fun of it, grab a stop watch and watch the time that it takes for the horse to "tire out" week after week. In time this exercise in futility will wear the owner out, not the horse. This is not groundwork. This is chaos, confusion, and counter productivity at its worst.

## Control vs. Chaos

Asking a horse to move specific body parts in a controlled manner is getting the horse to think, rather than react. Horses, by nature, are reactive animals—it's a survival skill. A horse sees something across the meadow that is unfamiliar, they snort and run thirty yards, stop, and reassess the situation. That is a prey animal's reactive response, and what has saved their lives for thousands of years. We are teaching them to behave in a way that is unnatural to them by asking them to think first and respond accordingly.

Using groundwork as a tool to exercise your horse's mind before a ride prepares the horse to listen to you, and gives you a chance to gage your horse's responsiveness to your cues and outside stimuli. Horses have off days, or crabby days, just like we do. On those days, it might take a little longer for your horse to listen and be responsive. You will spend a little extra time on the ground, to ensure a safe ride in the saddle. The next few pages illustrate some basic mind and body exercises that can get your horse focused on the task at hand.

To mix things up, take your horse outside of the arena or round pen, and do your groundwork in new areas. Poles, logs, water, tarps—be creative and break the monotony of a routine. Finding new ways to get your horse to think is not only fun for your horse, but fun for you as well. Obstacle courses are loads of fun, and there are books with practice patterns and ideas for fun things to do in your arena. If you don't have access to an arena, horse park, or obstacle course, you can set up your own in your pasture or woods.

When hiring a trainer, ask questions. Don't be fooled by the appearance of well-worn dirty boots, work gloves, and a "know-it-all" attitude. Ask for references. Ask to watch a few training sessions. If they won't allow spectators, find someone who will. Professional clinicians will come out and teach you to train your horse and provide private sessions. Group sessions are also offered to help share costs. Many times, it's not the horse that needs training, but the owner needs to learn to work with the horse effectively.

You need to have your horse's focus
on you to begin.

She is asking the horse to change directions by
stepping in front of the driveline.

In this photo, Karin is sending her horse to the left
and is getting the proper response.

AJ stops on a dime and turns at Karin's
request for a change of direction.

*Backing* is a great exercise that will help gain your horses respect and keep dominant, pushy horses out of your space. It is also very helpful for mouthy horses. Any time you have a horse that believes he is in charge, and very forward thinking, this is the go to exercise to help correct that kind of behavior. Do it everywhere and everyday for every horse.

# ~ Karin Roberts

Of the three gaited horses that I ride I would have to place AJ as my personal favorite. It's not because he is the smartest, prettiest, or even the smoothest horse to ride. Being that I'm a gaited horse gal, a smooth ride means everything. AJ is a Mangalarga Marchador horse. The Mangalarga Marchador breed is the national sport horse of Brazil, and currently there are only about two hundred of these horses in the US. They are known for their calm disposition, ability to excel in all disciplines, and smooth ambling gait. Those are the qualities that I look for in a gaited horse. As with every breed, there are always exceptions to the rule. AJ came to me as a three-year-old, and we have been working on smoothing out his gait for quite some time now. He is not naturally gaited and trots like a quarter horse. That's not a great thing when you ride gaited horses! What sets AJ apart from the rest of the herd is his willing attitude and his forgiving personality.

*"Sometimes it's not what you do to a horse that counts. It's what you don't do."*

*—Buster Mclaury*

Linda doesn't have a round pen, so she does her ground work in the paddock area.

Using the Downunder-horsemanship method, I have taught my horses to side pass on the ground as well as under saddle.

I often put various objects in the paddock to work with and to move around.

We always start and end our sessions with the flexing exercise. Flexing encourages softness. It helps them learn to give in to pressure. Learning this exercise was probably one of my favorite "aha" moments in my learning experience. When you can pick up on the reins with two fingers, and feel your horse give to the slightest request—there's just no greater feeling!"

"'Lateral flexion is the key to vertical flexion.'

—Clinton Anderson

Linda has a wooded pasture area that she has kept a few logs for jumping. During riding exercises, she uses the trees to circle around. Circling the trees helps the horse to focus and soften at the poll, neck, shoulders, and rib cage.

# ~ *Linda Gordon*

Tammi, Toby, and Allie—to say that they are my best friends would be an understatement. I have never dreamed of blue ribbons, breaking records for endurance, or competing at any level. When I first laid eyes on each of them they were skin and bone, mistreated, and left to die. My goal for them was to recover and survive. Once their health issues were resolved, the trust building began and progressed beyond what I could have imagined. With healthy bodies and minds, Tammi and Toby have gone back to the rescue farm on occasion when the farm hosts children with special needs. They stand patiently while being petted or mauled by hoards of little people who have never felt the softness of a horse's muzzle. Tammi seems to sense when a little person is placed on her back for their first ride. Her steps are slower, and she gently places each foot on the ground to ensure a safe ride. Toby, on the other hand, has a strong play drive and endless curiosity. He is always a source of great entertainment. I don't put young riders on his back, but he is affectionate and gentle on the ground. Allie, the newest of my little group, is a miniature mule who came to me at the age of fifteen. She wasn't handled much in her lifetime and used to run as fast as her little legs could carry her if you so much as looked in her direction. She has come a long way in her short time here, but still doesn't allow strangers to get too close.

Joan is longeing Lil' Dude over cavaletti jumps. You can build these jumps yourself and find the patterns on the internet. These are nice. By simply rolling it over, you can get three different heights for variety.

Here Joan is free longeing Tacoda in a thirty-six by fifty foot paddock. It's not necessary to have a round pen, any smaller enclosed space will do.

Yielding the hind quarters, you can see Tacoda's back right leg crossing her back left with just a look from Joan. Less dominant horses will turn and face the leader as a sign of respect.

Stepping out in front of the driveline will cause the horse to stop, turn, and change directions. Notice Tacoda's focus on Joan.

Turning on the haunches or yielding the forequarters. This is a great exercise for horses that are pushy with their front end.

# ~ *Joan Fischer*

Why mares? I have often been asked that question. With my interest being the breeding and starting of quarter horses, mares are an instrumental part of the process. I admire and respect their spirit. They have certain ideas that, at times, need expressing. Arizona and Cheyenne are my quarter mares. I also have an Arabian mare Tacoda who seemed to have found her way to me. I call her "The Misunderstood Arabian," her curiosity is a constant source of amusement—"The Littles" round out my herd. My miniature donkey, Mesa, came to us as a rescue that we are "fostering" (wink). She's not going anywhere. Dave may someday come to accept that. The Lil' Dude is my mini gelding that believes he is a stallion. He is the fierce guardian of his band of mares.

*"You get out of the horse what you put into the horse—the way you put it in."*
*—Ray Hunt*

Horses are afraid of anything that moves and makes a noise. Desensitizing is a great way to build their confidence and get them calm and thinking rather than reacting. When you introduce the object, keep the horses' head tipped toward you, but don't try to stop them from moving their feet. It's important to keep the pressure consistent until the horse stops moving its feet on its own and shows a sign of relaxing. Desensitizing exercises should be done between your sensitizing exercises. We use all kinds of fun tools to get the job done.

A little Easter flag from the dollar store tied to the end of the stick and string makes a great desensitizing object. It moves and makes a noise.

Linda is flapping an empty shavings bag on Toby's side. We started out by flapping the bag in the air first until he was comfortable with that, then we were able to flap the bag all over his body. All horses react differently, but with consistency, you'll have a very calm THINKING horse.

Linda finds great desensitizing objects at the local resale shop. Once the horses get comfortable with all kinds of different items, they get curious and playful and want to dominate the object. Just be sure to find things that can't hurt them and let the games begin!

In the photo above, Arizona is rolling around under the sprinkler on a hot sunny day. She has years of desensitization to scary objects to thank for her ability to enjoy a roll in the sprinkler. There is a right way and a wrong way to introduce new objects to your horse. The point of desensitizing is not to scare your horse to death, but rather to let him or her accept the new object willingly, using the thinking side of his or her brain. At first introduction to the plastic bag, tarp, or spray bottle (any scary-for-a-horse object) he may panic. The point at which you remove the "scary" object will be what teaches him the correct response to the situation. You don't want to shake a plastic bag, which will most likely cause your horse to panic, and then remove the bag because you don't like to see your horse get upset. You need to start out at a level that is mildly uncomfortable for your horse, and continue to apply the pressure until he relaxes and stands still. As your horse learns to accept this level of pressure, apply more pressure and again wait for him to relax. Once you've accomplished this on the left side, don't think your job is done. You've only taught the left side of your horse to accept the scary object, the right side of your horse has no idea what just happened. You'll need to desensitize the right side of your horse in the same manner as the left side. This all might sound easier than it is. It could take one horse five minutes to realize the bag isn't going to kill him while another horse might need a few days. You really have to keep your emotions (anger, temper, frustration) under control.

Toby's markings perfectly illustrate the horse's drive line. The white marking at the shoulder represents the drive line. Stepping in front of that line will cause the horse to slow or stop. Putting pressure behind that line will encourage the horse's forward movement.

The word groundwork might imply to some that it's "work" and, therefore, not much fun. Groundwork with my horses is probably my favorite pastime. We have *fun*! When I communicate an idea to my horses, and they understand what I'm asking them to do, there is no greater feeling in the world. I've learned the more I jump around, crawl all over them, and basically act like a lunatic, the more desensitized they get. Nothing I do surprises them anymore. Well, I guess that's not totally true.

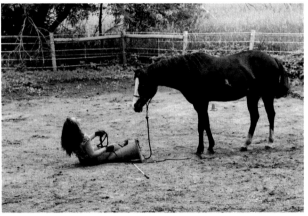

Tammi *was* a little surprised that I wasn't looking where I was going while I was running backwards. Who put that darn cone there anyway? As luck would have it, Joan was here using my camera to catch all the action! Don't repeat the same exercises day after day. Once your horse learns something, move on to something new to keep things interesting for your horse. Work your horse in different areas. Most importantly, make it fun for you and your horse.

# THE DREAM

## ~ *Linda Gordon*

I am racing across lush verdant fields. The stream is crystal clear, and the water tastes cool and clean. The sunlight gleams on my smooth slick coat, and the warm breeze dances through my mane and tail. I feel good and strong and healthy. Slowly, I wake to find that I've been dreaming again. I am stiff and sore; I am shivering from the cold and aching with hunger in this frozen pasture that I call home. I struggle to rise and join the others to find what nourishment I can. The hay is brown, moldy, and wet, but its all there is for us. Tempers are running short in the herd, and we fight to get close enough to the moldy hay for a bite or two before we are chased away by those that are stronger. I follow the fence line hoping to find a bit of brown grass on the other side, I stretch as far as I can, but I cannot reach far beyond the barbed wire. I see the little foal, born just days ago lying on the frozen ground, still, and motionless. Yesterday, he followed his mother as she tried to get close to the hay. Too close to the danger of striking hooves, he couldn't get out of the way quick enough, he hasn't moved since.

Evening is approaching, but I've lost all hope that someone might come to bring us fresh hay. It's been far too long; I don't think they're ever coming back. Another frigid night passes, another dream fades away. As a weak winter sun slants across the morning sky, I am barely able to stand. I stumble but somehow manage to get back on my feet. My coat is caked with dried mud, and there is a cold wind that seems to pass through my body and chills me to the bone. There was very little water left in the creek, and now it is frozen.

I hear a rumbling sound near the gate, as the rest of the herd stands motionless, ears forward, wary of the commotion. People are approaching; we stand cautious and ready to flee. Their eyes are kind, and they speak with voices that are soft and gentle. They move us forward toward the gate where the trucks and trailers await. Most of us are too weak to do anything but we follow where they lead. One by one, we step into the trailers, frightened and unsure. I feel a soft warm blanket surround me and I have a sense that. today, my life is about to change.

Winter and spring have passed, and I have not been hungry since that day in the frozen pasture when the trailers arrived. Each night, I lay in a dry soft bed that smells of pine, or with the earth beneath me, under the stars drifting off to sleep to the faint call of the whippoorwill.

I am racing across lush verdant fields. The streams are crystal clear and the water tastes cool and clean. The sunlight gleams on my smooth, slick coat, and the warm breeze dances through my mane and tail. I feel good and strong and healthy, I am no longer dreaming; I am loved.

# Tammi Before and After

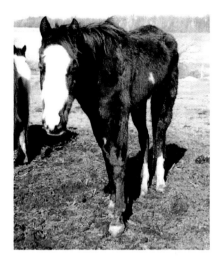

I would urge anybody looking for a horse to start with your local equine rescue organization. You will find just about any breed, any age ready for adoption. I personally have two horses and a miniature mule. All three once belonged to someone else and were starved and abandoned by their former owners. Not all horses living in rescue groups have been starved or abused. Many former owners have to relinquish their horses for various reasons; not every story is a tragic one. You will find your local rescue organizations on the web and you just might find the perfect equine partner waiting for you. Here is a partial list of recue organizations nationwide:

http://horse.rescueshelter.com/USA

*There is something about riding down the street on a prancing horse that makes you feel like something, even when you ain't a thing. ~ Will Rogers*

# BITS AND SPURS

Colt – Young male horse

Stallion – Male horse

Gelding – Male horse that has been castrated

Filly – Young female horse

Mare – Female horse

Foal – Newborn colt or filly

Weanling – Time in a foal's life from when they are weaned until they are a year old

Yearling – A one year old horse

Pedigree – Horses family tree

Papered horse – A horse that can prove its parentage and is *registered* with their breed's registry

Grade horse – An unregistered horse

Easy Keeper – A horse that gains weight easily and generally needs pasture time limited and grain withheld or receives a very small portion.

Difficult Keeper – The opposite of an easy keeper, think Jack Sprat and his wife

Started Under Saddle – Has begun training with saddle and rider

Green broke – A horse with limited experience under saddle

Dead Broke – Considered to be a very trustworthy, calm horse that has had a lot of experience under saddle. These make great husband horses

Hands (hh.) – The way to measure the height of the horse. The unit of measure originated before there was a set way of measurement. Using a man's hand they measured how many "hands" it was from the ground to the highest point of a horse's withers. Today a "hand" is four inches. So a horse that is fourteen and a half hands would be 14.2 or fourteen hands 2 inches

Hair Growth – The amount of daylight, not temperature determines when the horses will start growing their winter coat. You can have an early frosty day and find some of your horses shivering because they were not yet wearing their winter coat. On the opposite side of the spectrum, days might get shorter and signal growth but Indian summer might hang on and leave your horses uncomfortably hot

Chestnuts (not the roasting kind) – Also known as a night eye, is a callosity on the body of a horse found on the inner side of the leg above the knee on the front legs and below the hock on the hind leg. Evolution reduced the number of toes on the horse to one. The chestnut is thought to correspond with the wrist pad of dogs, or to be a vestigial scent gland. Chestnuts grow over time, if left alone, they will peel naturally

Lame – When a horse is injured and most likely is unable to be ridden

Sound – When a horse is healthy and able to be ridden without issue

Gaited Horse – Breeds that have natural gaited tendencies, that is, the ability to perform one of the smooth to ride, intermediate speed, four beat horse gaits

Muck rake – The rake designed to help with the never ending manure removal

Flek or "Flake" of hay – The small square portion of hay you pull off the bale

Hack – short, quick ride through the woods and/or fields

# Leg and Body markings

Stocking – White to the knee
Sock – White marking halfway up front or rear cannon.
Fetlock – White mark that extends over the fetlock joint.
Pastern – White mark that covers the pastern.
Coronet – A band of narrow white hair just above the top of the hoof.
Distal Spots – Dark spots within the white marking around the coronet.
Bendor Spots – Dark spots on the coat located anywhere on the body.
Watch Eye – Visible white around the iris of the eye as seen in the photo below.

# Face markings

Snip – Any white mark located between the nostrils (above)
Star – White marking on the forehead (above)
Stripe – White marking on the bridge of the nose
Blaze – Wider white marking that usually covers the region of the star stripe and snip but extends to the width of the bridge of the nose
Bald – A very wide blaze that extends to or may cover the eyes

mane
withers
back
loin
croup
tail
thigh
stifle
gaskin
hock
cannon
pastern
hoof
fetlock joint
coronet
fetlock
flank
belly
neck
shoulder
forearm
chest
elbow
knee
forelock
nose
cheek
nostril
lip
muzzle

www.visualdictionaryonline.com

*Small children are convinced that ponies
deserve to see the inside of the house.*
*~Maya Patel*

# HORSE CLASSIFIEDS DEFINITIONS

Event Prospect: Big, fast horse

Dressage Prospect – Big, slow horse

Pleasure Prospect – Pretty color

Sporting Prospect – Short, fast horse

Barrel Prospect – Fast horse which can turn

Endurance Prospect – Fast horse which will turn sometimes

Flashy – White sock

15:2 Hh – 14.3 hands high

16:2 Hh – 15:3 hands high

Big Trot – Can't canter within a two-mile straightaway

Nicely Started – Longes, but we don't have enough insurance to ride him yet

Bold – Runaway

Athletic – Runaway

Quiet – Lame on both front legs

Dead Quiet – Lame on all four legs

Good in Traffic (Bombproof) – Lame all around, deaf, and blind

Pony Type – Small and hairy

Arab Type – Looks startled

Thoroughbred Type – Looks terrified

Quarter Horse Type – Fat

Easy to Catch – Dead

Elegant – Thin

Black – Brown and/or dirty

Well–Mannered – Hasn't stepped on, run over, bit, or kicked anyone for a week

Professionally Trained – Hasn't stepped on, run over, bit or kicked anyone for a month

Clips, Hauls, Loads – "CLIPPITY, CLIPPITY" is the sound his hooves make as he "hauls" butt across the parking lot when you *try* to "load" him in the trailer.

Should Mature Sixteen Hands – Currently fourteen hands, dam is 14:2, sire is 14:3, every horse in his pedigree back eighteen generations is under fifteen hands, but *this* horse will defy his DNA and grow

To Loving Home Only – Expensive

To Show Home Only – Very Expensive

To Good Hone Only – Not really for sale unless you can (one) pay twice of what he is worth and (two) are willing to sign a 10-page legal document allowing current owner to tuck in beddy-bye every night

For Sale Due to lack of Time – Rider cannot afford to spend any more time in the hospital.

Any Vet Check Welcome – Please pay for us to find out what the #$^* is wrong with him

Recently Vetted – Someone else found something really wrong with this horse

Must Sell – Wife has left him and taken the kids

All Offers Considered – I am in traction for six months.

*"There is something about the outside of a horse that is good for the inside of a man."*
~ *Sir Winston Churchill*

*'Little Dude' and Mrs. Madeline Ronan ~ 2010*

There is something about the horse and its gentle nature that reaches out to us on a spiritual level. Equine therapy programs for children and adults with physical and mental challenges are being used throughout the world. The simple contact between horse and human has been known to bring autistic children to higher levels of communication, strengthen the physically handicapped, and provide a sense of peace to us all.

Lil' Dude recently made a home visit to Madeline, who suffers from Alzheimers.

A picture is worth a thousand words.

# Spring

It's a great time of year to do some spring cleaning in the barn and pastures. While the spring rains are falling, there is no reason you can't hang out in the barn and clean and oil your tack, check for worn straps and tighten those pesky Chicago screws on your reins and bridles.

# Summer

Be prepared for those annoying summer bugs. They are hungry, and your horses are just the meal they have been dreaming about. Fly spray is one of those things you don't want to run out of over the summer months. Be sure to keep your water tanks clean and full of cool water to drink. Tanks should not be a breeding ground for bugs and tadpoles. Keeping a couple of fans in the barn is a nice way to keep your horses comfortable on those hot, sticky summer afternoons.

# Fall

It's time to make sure your tank heaters are in good working order and that your darlings haven't left teeth marks in the cord from last year. It's also a good time to check your winter blankets for torn straps and broken buckles. Fill your barn with hay now and avoid the possibility of inclement weather or shortage of hay.

# Winter

If you live in a snowy environment, there are times that the snow is falling faster than the manure can be picked up. Not all horse activity has to stop just because a little snow falls, or a lot depending on where you live. It's a great time to practice patterns in your pasture. It's also a really nice time of year to brush up on your bareback skills—thick fluffy snow makes for a soft landing. While spending extra time indoors to avoid frostbite, you can evaluate and set new goals for the coming year.

"There is a special bond between human and horse.
There is a mutual trust and respect that develops
when you let them know you're in charge and they
are okay with that".

# BLUNDERS, BLOOPERS, AND MISHAPS

## ~ *Joan Fischer*

I was working my two year old, Providence, on a longe line in my arena. I was using a fairly long rope but had a good portion of it on the ground. Things were going really well until she got the idea that she needed to bolt over to the gate to see her girlfriends. The rope tightened around my boot and pulled me right off my feet. I was dumped unceremoniously onto my hindquarters in the dirt. The rope then yanked the boot right off my foot. Providence began to panic as she realized she was being chased by a boot type predator. She ran at high speed around the arena trying to evade the killer boot. She gradually began to slow down, and I could see the thinking part of her brain regaining control over the reactive side. She stopped and turned to bravely face the enemy. She approached with caution, sniffed the boot and looked directly at me. I guess getting a whiff of my scent reminded her that I was supposed to be a part of this equation.

## ~ *Pam Zeidman*

Early on in my horse ownership experience, I would take both of my mares for a ride through the neighborhood. I would ride one and pony the other. One day in early spring, I was riding Sydney and had Aussie on the lead rope, which was tied around my saddle horn (mistake number one). We were wandering around my neighbor's property when we came to a small gully that Sydney was a little unsure of. When I thought she decided it was okay, instead of walking across, she jumped it. Aussie was not going to have any part of this gully jumping and pulled back. With me caught in the middle of my horses' to jump or not to jump argument, it was only logical that since we were tied together by the horn, something had to give. The saddle horn popped off, and so did I; I landed to the side of the gully flat on my back, bounced the back of my head off the ground (no helmet. Mistake number two) and laid there for a few minutes to catch my breath. Both horses were looking down at me and had to be wondering why I was looking back up at them. I finally got to my feet and led them back home. The saddle was eventually repaired—it is now a hornless saddle.

## ~ *Tanya Newkirk*

Most of my mishaps with horses are caused by me and my carelessness; trying to rush things when dealing with a horse seldom works out well. One evening I was trying to hurry up and throw my bareback pad on my mare. My niece was already riding one of our other horses, and I decided to jump on my mare and join her. My horse was tied to a post in a run that had metal pipes for rails. I had thrown the pad over her, grabbed the cinch and buckled it loosely. She was standing parallel to the fence, and I asked her to move away from the fence so I could make sure the cinch wasn't twisted. We had a small problem that I managed to make larger. She started to move and stopped, so I asked her to move again with a little more insistence this time. In my hurry, I hadn't notice that she was so close to the fence and that I had managed to fasten her to the top rail by the cinch. She panicked, and, of course, being so horse savvy, I joined in her state of panic. She did calm down without getting hurt, but not until the strap broke as well as five wooden posts in the run. Guess what we did the next day?

## ~ *Linda Gordon*

I just can't seem to pass my barn without stopping to snuggle my horses. Yes, I said it, I snuggle my horses. It doesn't matter how I'm dressed, I guess the smell of horse is like perfume to me. One particular evening, I returned from dinner and stopped by the barn. I was wearing a sweater jacket that hung past my knees, a lovely beaded pair of jeans and boots with a two inch heal. Not exactly riding attire, but that wasn't important. I was only planning on giving her what I call "our full body hug." Without a halter or rope, I pulled the mounting block over to Tammi and threw my leg over her back. Usually, this is not a problem. This time though, my fancy two-inch heeled boot got caught up in my fancy long sweater jacket, and I found myself in a tangled mess. At first, she was okay with all the extra wiggling I was doing while trying to dislodge my boot from my sweater. The wiggling caused me to lose my balance and at this point I am flopping, kicking, and cursing as my predicament worsened. Tammi lost her patience with my wardrobe malfunction and she decided to flee the scene. I was lying on top of her and flopping around like a fish out of water as she sped up, I squeezed tighter, effectively asking her to go faster. Needless to say, I ended up ruining my favorite beaded jeans, and ripping that fancy sweater when I hit the ground in a mangled ball of yarn, denim, and leather. We still have our full body hugs. I just make sure that I'm not wearing anything that I can get tangled up in first.

# LONGMEADOW RESCUE RANCH

Nestled among 165 acres of woodland near Union, Missouri, the Humane Society of Missouri's Longmeadow Ranch is a state-of-the-art haven for hundreds of horses, cows, goats, pigs, ducks, and other farm animals rescued from abuse and neglect. The ranch, established in 1988, is one of the most comprehensive horse and farm animal rescue, rehabilitation, and adoption centers in the country. In addition to animal care, our ranch staff provides hands-on humane education experiences for both children and adults. The ranch also offers an animal sponsorship program called Barn Buddies which helps provide food, board, and medical care for Longmeadow animals. Sponsors at the fifty-dollar level receive a plush animal replica of their Barn Buddy. Persons interested in meeting adoptable animals or their Barn Buddies can visit the ranch on Fridays and Saturdays or by appointment on other days.

Please visit: www.longmeadowrescueranch.org for more information.

# A MAN AND HIS HORSE

In St. Louis, Missouri, at the Kraus Farm boarding stable, horse owners are buzzing around the barn, preparing for a ride on a gloriously warm spring day. As riders lead their horses down the aisle, the sound of horses' hooves on concrete echoes throughout the barn, punctuated by the occasional soft whinny—music to a horse lover's ears.

In the last stall on the right, Frosty hears the unmistakable shuffling gait of his friends approach. His ears prick forward as he turns toward the stall door, and waits for Dale to greet him with soft, kind words and the gentle stroke of his hand. Dale Ludwig, now 73, and Frosty, age 29, ride the trails together six days a week. That kind of dedication is rare and impressive by any equestrian's standards, but that's only the beginning of the story.

Dales' love of horses began around the age of ten, when his father bought a farm in Hawk Point, Missouri. He enjoyed riding throughout his childhood and into his adult life, until a stroke changed everything at the age of fifty-two. With the use of his right side severely limited, Dale's life would change forever, but horses were never far from his thoughts. Five years after his stroke, it was his daughter who helped him find the perfect horse for his special needs.

In 1996, Frosty, a fourteen year old Appaloosa

gelding, was known to be sure footed and steady on the trails. Frosty seemed to know that Dale needed special care, and compensated for Dales limited mobility. When mounting, Frosty stands patiently, without moving a muscle, to allow Dale the time he needs to get in the saddle safely. Once mounted, the trusted gelding carries Dale down the trail. Only on horseback can Dale move uninhibited and free at whatever pace he chooses. Wandering through the forested hills of Missouri, across streams, and up to the high bluffs where the breathtaking views had been out of reach since his stroke.

It wasn't long before Dale and Frosty joined up with a group of trail riders at Kraus Farm known as The Wild Bunch. As described by the name, these rambunctious riders enjoyed a fast paced jaunt through the countryside.

Dale's eyes twinkled as he spoke of the camaraderie of the group and of the many great rides they shared. As many as twenty-five riders spent hours together enjoying the trails and each other's company. Dale's physical limitations were of no consequence, Frosty was more than capable of keeping up with the group and kept Dale safe at the walk, trot, canter, and the gallop. Many years have passed, and most members of the wild bunch are gone now, but fond memories still remain.

By the age of twenty-six, Frosty had gradually lost vision in both of his eyes. For thirteen years, Frosty willingly and faithfully carried his friend across rugged terrain on strong, steady legs. Sir Winston Churchill said, "There is something about the outside of a horse that is good for the inside of a man." Dale knows no truer words have ever been spoken. Love, loyalty, and trust—such simple words seem inadequate when describing the bond between this man and this horse. With slow and deliberate effort to speak, Dale said, "I depend on his legs, and he depends on my eyes." Because of his blindness, Frosty can no longer be turned out with the rest of the herd. Often times, a blind horse turned out to pasture with a herd falls victim to the social hierarchy and finds himself at the bottom of the pecking order. It only takes one sighted horse to challenge the blind one, causing him to flee in a panic. Without sight, the blind horse is likely to run into a tree or a fence causing injury or even death. With Frosty's safety and well-being in mind, Dale arrives at the barn everyday to care for him. Unable to use his

right arm, and slightly dragging his right leg, Dale leads Frosty to the grass to graze.

It's been said that horses restore the human spirit and make the impossible possible. The profound sense of trust these two friends have in one another is nothing short of miraculous. Six days a week, Frosty waits to hear the sound of his friend's unmistakable shuffling gait as he approaches. Dale opens the tack box he built just a few years back to retrieve a brush and curry comb. He speaks to Frosty in a soft voice as the brush gently glides over his sleek coat to remove bits of shavings before tacking up. With his tack in his left hand, his right arm pressed to his side, and in one swift motion, Dale places the saddle pad then the saddle on Frosty's back. Frosty lowers his head to accept the bridle, and in moments, the pair is ready to ride the trails as they have done for years.

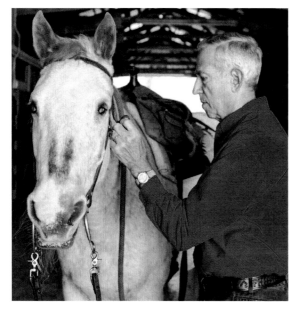

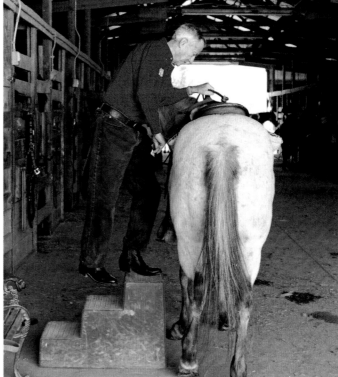

*"In riding a horse we borrow freedom."*

—*Helen Thomas*